RELEASING THE ANOINTING OFFICIAL WORKBOOK

JAMES TAN

Harrison House

Harrison House P.O. Box 310, Shippensburg, PA 17257-0310

This book and all other Harrison House's books are available at Christian bookstores and distributors worldwide.

For Worldwide Distribution.

Reach us on the Internet: www.harrisonhouse.com.

ISBN 13 TP: 9781667510149

ISBN 13 eBook: 9781667510156

CONTENTS

INTRODUCTION TO "RELEASING THE ANOINTING: OFFICIAL WORKBOOK"

Welcome to the "Releasing the Anointing: Official Workbook," a transformative guide designed to deepen your understanding of God's dynamic power within you and how to actively engage with it in your daily spiritual journey. This workbook is a companion to the teachings that delve into the profound subject of the Holy Spirit's anointing—the divine enablement that empowers believers to fulfill their God-given destinies. Here, you'll find a structured pathway that draws from biblical insights and practical steps, inviting you to explore, reflect, and apply the principles discussed in each chapter.

KEY TAKEAWAYS AND EXPECTATIONS

- **Understanding the Fivefold Ministry**: One of the core teachings of this workbook revolves around the fivefold ministry—apostles, prophets, evangelists, pastors, and teachers—and their vital roles within the Body of Christ. You will learn how each of these ministries is essential for the church's health and growth, providing stability and direction as we pursue the fullness of Christ together.

- **Deepening Your Worship Experience**: Worship is more than music; it's a posture of the heart that honors God. This workbook encourages you to transcend traditional views of worship, urging you to engage in a more profound and meaningful relationship with God through adoration that goes beyond the surface level of contemporary worship practices.

- **Exploring Corporate and Individual Anointing**: Discover the power of corporate anointing that manifests when believers unite in worship and prayer, alongside understanding how individual anointing operates to influence your personal walk with God. These insights aim to enhance both your personal spiritual life and your contribution to the communal aspects of faith.

- **Practical Engagement with the Spiritual Gifts**: This workbook does not just discuss spiritual gifts in theory but prompts you to identify, activate, and cultivate these gifts in your life. Through reflective questions and actionable steps, you're invited to engage actively with your inherent spiritual capacities, enriching both your life and those around you.

- **Strategies for Spiritual Growth and Leadership**: Leadership in a spiritual context is about influence, stewardship, and alignment with God's divine order. You will explore the characteristics of godly leadership and learn how to apply these in various areas of life and ministry, ensuring that you are building on a foundation that honors God and expands His kingdom.

- **Facilitating Divine Encounters**: Through structured guidance, this workbook helps you create environments—both personally and within your community—that are conducive to divine encounters. Whether it's through setting up a prayer room at home or organizing corporate prayer meetings, you're equipped to foster spaces where the Holy Spirit's presence is vividly experienced.

- **Nurturing a Heart for Intercession**: A significant portion of this workbook is dedicated to developing a powerful intercessory prayer life. You'll be taught how to stand in the gap for others effectively, understanding the principles of spiritual warfare and the responsibility that comes with it.

- **Cultivating Unity in the Body of Christ**: Unity is not just a theological ideal but a practical necessity for the church's health. This workbook provides practical advice on fostering unity within your local church community, emphasizing the strength and beauty of diverse members working together in harmony.

- **In-depth Biblical Foundation**: Each chapter is rooted in Scripture, providing you with a deep biblical foundation for every concept discussed. This approach ensures that your growth and learning are anchored in the truth of God's Word.

- **Continuous Spiritual Development**: Lastly, this workbook is designed not just for temporary growth but for continuous spiritual development. The lessons, practices, and insights are intended to be revisited and applied throughout your spiritual journey, adapting to each stage of your growth.

WHAT YOU CAN EXPECT TO RECEIVE

As you embark on this journey with the "Releasing the Anointing: Official Workbook," expect to be challenged, inspired, and transformed. This workbook is designed not only to impart knowledge but to facilitate a deep, experiential understanding of living under God's anointing. Each page invites you into a deeper communion with the Holy Spirit, encouraging you to live a life marked by divine power and purpose.

Prepare to dive deep, pray earnestly, and worship passionately as you unlock the full potential of the anointing in your life. Whether you are a new believer or a seasoned leader, this workbook offers you the tools to significantly impact your spiritual life and the lives of those you influence.

Welcome to a journey of profound transformation—one that promises to elevate your relationship with God and empower you to walk in the fullness of His anointing. Let's begin this sacred adventure together, expecting nothing less than a life-changing encounter with the Spirit of God.

∾

CHAPTER I

ANOINTED TO KNOW THE ANOINTING

The Holy Spirit is not only a gift from God but also a mark of His everlasting covenant with you. Remember, "the anointing which you have received from Him abides in you" (1 John 2:27, NKJV). You are never alone, and you are always empowered.

"The anointing which you have received from Him abides in you, and you do not need that anyone teach you; but as the same anointing teaches you concerning all things, and is true, and is not a lie, and just as it has taught you, you will abide in Him." - 1 John 2:27 (NKJV)

In the exploration of the anointing, we discern both continuity and distinction between the manifestations of the Holy Spirit in the Old and New Testaments. **Old Testament vs. New Testament Anointing** reveals that historically, the Spirit's presence was selectively temporary, designated primarily for prophets, kings, and priests to empower them for specific divine missions. This temporary anointing lifted once the designated tasks were completed. The radical transformation under the New Covenant, introduced through Jesus' sacrifice, ushered in a revolutionary change: the Holy Spirit now permanently **indwells believers**, making us the living temples of God's Spirit. This indwelling signifies a profound shift from the Old Testament practices where the presence of God was sought externally, to the New Testament reality where we carry His presence within us.

This transformation is rooted deeply in the powerful, redemptive work of Jesus Christ. The shedding of His blood did more than cleanse us; it removed our Adamic sin nature and reinstated our spiritual essence, enabling the Holy Spirit to dwell within us. This is the essence of the **Indwelling of the Holy Spirit**—a gift that marks us permanently as God's own, transforming us into carriers of His divine presence wherever we go, liberated from the constraints of seeking God in a specific locale.

Understanding the context of prayers in the Bible sheds light on the relational dynamics between God and humanity across covenants. When we read the psalmist's plea, "Do not cast me away from Your presence, and do not take Your Holy Spirit from me" (Psalms 51:11), it echoes the Old Covenant's conditional engagement with the Spirit. This highlights the **Covenantal Prayer in Context**; a stark contrast to the permanence of the Spirit's indwelling under the New Covenant, where even in transgression, the Spirit remains with us, committed to restoring and guiding us back to righteousness.

The purpose of the Holy Spirit's indwelling goes beyond mere companionship; it includes **Transformation through the Holy Spirit**. This transformation is both ethical and spiritual, empowering us not only to avoid sin but to actively embody holiness. The Spirit shapes our inner lives, molding our character to reflect divine attributes, and enhancing our capacity to experience and distribute God's love and truth in the world around us.

The Scripture delineates various **Gifts and Anointings for**

Service, illustrating how the Spirit equips the church for diverse functions. From the motivational gifts in Romans 12, aimed at strengthening the local church, to the ministerial gifts in Ephesians for broader church and societal edification, and the supernatural gifts in 1 Corinthians designed for both local and global impact, these gifts embody the full spectrum of Christ's earthly ministry. Each believer is imbued with these gifts not just for personal edification but for the collective upliftment of the body of Christ.

The Purpose of Anointing in our lives is dual-fold: it consecrates and empowers us. Being set apart for God's use involves more than just being chosen; it means being equipped and empowered to undertake God's assignments with divine authority and power. This anointing marks us distinctly in the world as God's emissaries, tasked with specific kingdom mandates.

In the fabric of the kingdom, **Anointing to Serve** plays a critical role. True ministry, modeled by Christ, is not about elevation or status but about service. This anointing calls us into the humility and sacrifice of serving others, reflecting Jesus' life who came not to be served but to serve. This service, which often looks like simple acts of kindness and practical help, is where our spiritual maturity is tested and grown.

However, the anointing is not just for outward service; it also sustains us. The **Sustaining Anointing** ensures that our inner lives are nourished and that we continue in our spiritual journey without faltering. This aspect of the anointing preserves us, empowering us to endure and persevere through challenges without losing our faith or effectiveness in ministry.

On a personal level, the anointing fosters our spiritual development. **The Anointing in Personal Growth** encourages us to delve deeper into our relationship with God, enhancing our understanding of His will and aligning our lives more closely with His purposes. This growth is not passive; it requires active engagement with the Holy Spirit through prayer, meditation on the Scriptures, and obedient response to His promptings.

Lastly, the anointing opens our eyes to the beauty of Christ. **Anointing for Intimacy and Revelation** allows us to behold Jesus as in a mirror, transforming us into His image from glory to glory. This anointing draws us into deeper communion with God, revealing His character and will, making our journey not just one of following rules but of engaging in a loving relationship with the Creator.

REFLECTIVE QUESTIONS

1. How does understanding the permanence of the Holy Spirit's indwelling impact your view of God's presence in your life?
2. Reflect on a time when you experienced the Holy Spirit guiding or correcting you. What did you learn from that experience?
3. In what ways can you more effectively utilize the gifts of the Spirit in your community or church?
4. How does the concept of the Holy Spirit's sustaining anointing change your approach to ministry and personal spiritual disciplines?
5. What steps can you take to cultivate a deeper intimacy with God, allowing the Holy Spirit to transform you more into the image of Christ?

ACTIONABLE STEPS

- **Cultivate an Awareness of the Holy Spirit**: Start each day with a prayer inviting the Holy Spirit to open your eyes and heart to His presence and guidance throughout the day.
- **Equip Yourself with Knowledge of the Gifts**: Study the spiritual gifts listed in Romans 12, 1 Corinthians 12, and Ephesians 4. Identify which gifts you may have and seek ways to develop and use them in your life and your church.
- **Engage in Service**: Find a service opportunity in your church or community that aligns with your spiritual gifts. Commit to regular involvement, using your gifts to serve others and build up the body of Christ.

JOURNALING **Prompt**

Reflect on the concept of being "the temple of the Holy Spirit." How does this understanding change your daily life, your interactions with others, and your personal spiritual practices? Write about the ways you can honor this divine indwelling in everyday actions and decisions.

~

_____
_____
_____
_____
_____
_____
_____
_____
_____
_____
_____
_____
_____
_____
_____
_____
_____
_____
_____
_____
_____
_____
_____
_____
_____
_____
_____
_____
_____
_____
_____
_____

CHAPTER 2
A KNOWING ANOINTING

Remember, you carry a divine anointing that goes beyond human wisdom and strength. Let this assurance dwell richly in you, empowering you to live and move with confidence in your God-given abilities and insights.

"But you have an anointing from the Holy One, and you know all things." - 1 John 2:20 (NKJV)

Understanding the anointing requires us to grasp that it is multifaceted, deeply woven into every aspect of a believer's life. This is not a mere emotional stir; it encompasses wisdom, knowledge, and practical application. The **Holistic Function of the Anointing** shows us that while it can indeed touch our emotions, its primary role extends much further, providing guidance, instruction, and empowerment for a variety of life's situations.

As we delve into the specific roles of the anointing, we see that a primary aspect is its ability to offer **Guidance and Instruction**. This aligns with the promises Jesus made about the

Holy Spirit, that He would teach us all things and remind us of everything Jesus said. This promise isn't just for spiritual knowledge but includes wisdom for our daily lives, helping us make decisions that align with God's will.

The diversity within the unity of the anointing is akin to the variety of sports under the single banner of the Olympic Games. This analogy helps us understand the **Unity and Diversity of the Anointing**—one Spirit manifesting through varied gifts and operations, tailored to the needs and callings of each believer. Just as athletes specialize in different sports but compete in the same games, believers operate under the same anointing but manifest it through different gifts and ministries.

Reflecting on the **Symbolism of Anointing Oil** used in the Old Testament, which was applied to consecrate everything from Tabernacle articles to kings and priests, helps us appreciate that the same Holy Spirit empowers us for diverse roles within God's kingdom. The oil, a symbol of the Holy Spirit, was not different for each anointing; similarly, the Holy Spirit adapts His work to each of our callings without changing His essence.

This understanding leads us to recognize the importance of **Specialization in Anointing**. Like the craftsmen Bezalel and Aholiab, who were anointed specifically for artistic workmanship, we too are equipped in areas that align with our divine purpose. Each of us must identify and hone the particular anointing we carry, becoming skilled in cooperating with the Holy Spirit in our specific domains.

The encouragement to **Work with Your Anointing** challenges us to actively engage with the Holy Spirit's empowerment in our daily tasks and ministries. This means not just acknowledging our gifts but actively developing and using them to fulfill God's purposes, enhancing both our lives and those around us.

The reality of the **Inherent Anointing in Believers** is profound. John tells us we have received an anointing from the

Holy One, and it resides within us—not in some distant future but here and now. This anointing is a present, active reality in the life of every believer, a source of power and guidance.

One of the most practical aspects of the anointing is its **Protective and Directional Function.** It acts almost like a spiritual compass, guiding us away from harm and steering us towards opportunities where we can effectively serve God's purposes. This function is essential for maintaining our spiritual health and effectiveness.

In my ministry, I've often seen how the **Anointing's Role in Discernment** is crucial, especially in complex spiritual environments. Just like Paul's interaction with the slave girl possessed by a spirit of divination, the anointing provides us with the discernment to recognize not only the surface truths but also the spiritual realities that underlie them.

Lastly, the significance of the **Everyday Guidance of the Anointing** cannot be overstated. This guidance is not reserved for monumental life decisions or pivotal ministry moments alone. Rather, it permeates the everyday, mundane choices we make, proving that the Holy Spirit is interested in every detail of our lives.

REFLECTIVE QUESTIONS

1. In what ways have you experienced the guiding aspect of the anointing in your personal decisions?
2. How can you more effectively recognize and operate in the specific anointing God has given you?
3. Reflect on a time when the Holy Spirit guided you away from a potentially harmful situation. What did you learn?

4. How does understanding the unity and diversity of the anointing change your perception of the Holy Spirit's work in the church?
5. What steps can you take to cultivate a deeper sensitivity to the anointing's protective and directional functions?

ACTIONABLE STEPS

- **Cultivate Sensitivity to the Holy Spirit**: Begin each day with a prayer for heightened sensitivity to the Holy Spirit's guidance in every decision and interaction throughout your day.
- **Equip Yourself with Knowledge of Your Gifts**: Take time to study the spiritual gifts in the New Testament. Seek understanding and training in the gifts you feel particularly drawn to or have been affirmed in by others.
- **Engage with Others in Your Anointed Area**: Find or create opportunities to use your anointed gifts in service to others, whether in your local church, community, or workplace. This could be through teaching, counseling, arts, or any area where you feel the Spirit's empowerment.

JOURNALING Prompt

Reflect on how the anointing has manifested in your life in both usual and unusual ways. Consider the different situations where you have felt the Holy Spirit's guidance or intervention. Write about these experiences and how they have shaped your understanding of God's presence and power in your life.

~

CHAPTER 3
THE ANOINTING TEACHES US

Hold onto the truth that the anointing within you is a direct line to God's wisdom and guidance. Let this fill you with peace and confidence as you navigate your spiritual journey.

"But the Helper, the Holy Spirit, whom the Father will send in My name, He will teach you all things, and bring to your remembrance all things that I said to you." - John 14:26 (NKJV)

The **Dynamic Roles of the Anointing** in our spiritual education emphasize that growth in God involves both a deep, living connection with the Word and intimate ongoing communication with the Holy Spirit. The anointing teaches and guides, reminding us of God's words and illuminating our path as we apply these truths in our lives.

Understanding that the **Anointing Teaches Through Various Methods** helps us appreciate its comprehensive role in our spiritual lives. It not only recalls the Word to our memory but also enlightens us during our study, preaching, and personal revelations. This diverse functionality ensures that we are equipped for every aspect of life and ministry.

The **Ministry of the Holy Spirit as Teacher** signifies the importance God places on instruction. It's reassuring to know that the Spirit is committed to our education, ensuring we grasp the deeper meanings and applications of biblical truths. This teaching role of the Holy Spirit is fundamental to our spiritual growth and ability to navigate life's challenges.

Reflecting on the **Memorial Function of the Anointing**, we recognize that it not only aids in remembering scriptural truths but also enhances our cognitive and spiritual recall during ministry. This aspect is crucial, as demonstrated by the apostle Peter's sermon at Pentecost, where he was inspired to quote and explain Scripture extensively and effectively.

The **Unifying Power of the Anointing** in the early church highlights the collective strength and harmony that the Holy Spirit fosters among believers. This unity is essential for a potent move of the Spirit, which is hindered by disunity and individualistic pursuits.

The anointing's **Role in Illumination** cannot be overstated. It opens our spiritual eyes, allowing us to see beyond the immediate and obvious, to grasp the deeper spiritual realities. This illumination often comes through direct revelation or through serendipitous encounters that provide clarity and understanding.

In **Spirit-Led Instruction**, the Holy Spirit directly imparts wisdom and insight, bypassing conventional learning methods. This direct teaching can occur in moments of prayer, worship, or even in everyday activities, emphasizing that the Spirit is continually speaking to us.

The **Corporate Dimension of Anointing** teaches us that while we have personal access to the anointing, there is a powerful dynamic that unfolds when we come together. The collective anointing within a community can lead to profound spiritual insights and breakthroughs.

The **Anointing's Personal Touch** is evident when the Holy Spirit tailors His teachings to our individual journeys. This personalized instruction is designed to guide us into all truth, making our path clear and our decisions aligned with God's will.

Lastly, the **Ongoing Dialogue with the Spirit** underscores that the anointing is not a one-time event but a continuous interaction with the Holy Spirit. This daily communication is vital for maintaining our spiritual health and for making constant adjustments to our course according to His guidance.

REFLECTIVE QUESTIONS

1. How has the Holy Spirit used the anointing to teach you in a specific instance?
2. In what ways can you improve your sensitivity to the anointing's guidance and teaching?
3. How does understanding the anointing's role in unity affect your approach to church and community life?
4. Reflect on a moment when the anointing brought a Scripture or truth vividly to your remembrance. What impact did it have on your life or ministry at the time?
5. How can you cultivate a more consistent dialogue with the Holy Spirit in your daily routine?

ACTIONABLE STEPS

- **Cultivate a Daily Discipline**: Start each day with Scripture reading followed by a prayer for the Holy

Spirit to illuminate the words you read and apply them to your daily circumstances.

- **Equip Yourself with Spiritual Sensitivity:** Engage in regular spiritual practices such as fasting, silent meditation, and other disciplines that enhance your sensitivity to the Holy Spirit's voice.
- **Engage in Community Worship:** Actively participate in your church's worship services and small groups to experience and contribute to the corporate anointing.

JOURNALING **Prompt**

Reflect on how the anointing has taught you in personal, unexpected ways. Write about instances where you felt the Holy Spirit guiding you through a difficult decision or opening your understanding to new spiritual insights. How did these experiences deepen your relationship with God?

∾

_____

_____

_____

_____

_____

_____

_____

_____

_____

_____

_____

_____

_____

_____

_____

_____

_____

_____

_____

_____

_____

_____

_____

_____

_____

_____

_____

_____

_____

CHAPTER 4
ANOINTED FOR LIFE

Encourage yourself in the Lord, for He has already equipped you for every challenge. Lean into His presence, and the Holy Spirit will unfold the wisdom and strength you need each step of the way.

But the Helper, the Holy Spirit, whom the Father will send in My name, He will teach you all things, and bring to your remembrance all things that I have said to you (John 14:26).

As we journey together in understanding the profound work of the Holy Spirit in our lives, let us consider the **Eternal Perspective of Our Earthly Walk**. We must remember that our earthly existence is not merely a passage of time but the commencement of an eternal relationship with God. This divine relationship begins here and now and extends into eternity. Every day is significant because it's a stepping stone into a timeless fellowship with our Creator.

In every aspect of our daily lives, whether mundane or monumental, we are **Anointed for Life**. This anointing is not a tool reserved for emergencies; it is a daily companion that influences every decision, action, and interaction. It is through this anointing that the Holy Spirit manifests His presence, making the ordinary sacred and the mundane meaningful.

It's important to recognize that our walk with the Holy Spirit demands that we **Walk in the Anointing Every Day**. This commitment transforms our ordinary days into extraordinary testimonies of God's ongoing work in our lives. Like David, who was prepared for Goliath by facing lions and bears in his daily duties, we too are prepared for bigger battles through the faithful execution of our daily tasks.

This brings us to the understanding that **God in His Mercy Only Allows Progressive Giants**. Our challenges in life are never random; they are carefully orchestrated by God to build us up progressively. Just as David faced a lion and then a bear before confronting Goliath, we face increasing challenges that are matched by an increasing measure of God's grace and anointing.

To fully embrace this daily anointing, we must understand that the **Anointing Is Not Just for Emergencies**. If we only seek the Holy Spirit's power in times of crisis, we miss out on the fullness of His presence in all aspects of life. Living in this truth helps us navigate every circumstance with divine strength and wisdom.

Furthermore, the **Anointing Teaches Us** in our daily encounters. As we engage with the world around us, the Holy Spirit teaches us through every interaction, guiding us to reflect Christ in our thoughts, words, and actions. This daily teaching is vital as it shapes our character and deepens our relationship with God.

The role of the **Renewed Mind in an Anointed Life** cannot be overstated. A mind renewed by the Word and the Spirit thinks, judges, and acts in accordance with God's will. This renewal is essential for living out the fullness of the anointing, preventing us from falling into erratic behaviors that do not glorify God.

Indeed, the **Wisdom of God Teaches Us First in Private.** Our private victories and lessons equip us for public challenges and successes. By growing in the anointing in solitude, we are strengthened to stand firm and shine brightly in the public eye, maintaining our integrity and purpose.

It's crucial to remember that **Training in the Anointing** prepares us for future challenges. Just as athletes train off the field, believers must cultivate their spiritual strength daily. This training involves not just spiritual disciplines but also a heart posture that is responsive to the Holy Spirit's guidance.

Lastly, the anointing reinforces that **When Believers Try to Skip Forward to Demonstrations of Power Without Allowing the Anointing to Grow Them, It Tilts Them Off Balance.** Spiritual maturity involves a balance of power and character, which comes from a deep, ongoing engagement with the Holy Spirit.

REFLECTIVE QUESTIONS

1. How does your daily routine reflect a life anointed by the Holy Spirit?
2. In what ways can you recognize the progressive challenges God has placed in your life to prepare you for greater battles?
3. How do you integrate the Holy Spirit's teachings into your everyday decisions?
4. In what ways has a renewed mind changed how you react to situations compared to before you were walking in the anointing?
5. What practices help you maintain a sensitivity to the Holy Spirit's guidance?

. . .

ACTIONABLE STEPS

- **Cultivate** a daily discipline of prayer and reading the Word to keep your spirit attuned to the Holy Spirit's promptings.
- **Equip** yourself with knowledge of the Word which acts as the foundation for discerning the Holy Spirit's voice against the noise of the world.
- **Engage** in regular spiritual check-ups by reflecting on your actions and attitudes, ensuring they align with the character and nature of Christ as revealed by the Holy Spirit.

JOURNALING **Prompt**

Reflect on a recent situation where you felt the anointing guide you in a decision. How did you recognize the Holy Spirit's influence, and what was the outcome? How does this experience encourage you to be more attentive to His guidance in the future?

～

_____

_____

_____

_____

_____

_____

_____

_____

_____

_____

_____

_____

_____

_____

_____

_____

_____

_____

_____

_____

_____

_____

_____

_____

_____

_____

_____

_____

_____

_____

CHAPTER 5
SALT AND LIGHT

Embrace your role as salt and light in the world. Let your daily actions be a testament to God's transformative power in your life, manifesting His love and righteousness in every interaction.

"You are the salt of the earth; but if the salt loses its flavor, how shall it be seasoned? It is then good for nothing but to be thrown out and trampled underfoot by men. You are the light of the world. A city that is set on a hill cannot be hidden. Nor do they light a lamp and put it under a basket, but on a lampstand, and it gives light to all who are in the house. Let your light so shine before men, that they may see your good works and glorify your Father in heaven."
(Matthew 5:13-16 NKJV).

As we delve into the profound impact of the Holy Spirit in our lives, it's vital to grasp that our anointing as believers is not merely for our benefit but also to influence those around us profoundly. This influence extends **beyond**

the four walls of the church and into every area where we have the privilege to represent Christ.

The anointing we carry is not limited to moments of spiritual highs or church services; it is meant for every sphere of life where God has placed us. As **salt and light**, we are empowered to preserve goodness and illuminate darkness in our surroundings through the divine enablement of the Holy Spirit. This is our identity and mission—to impact and transform our world actively.

Understanding our role as God's ambassadors means recognizing that **the anointing should go wider**, touching all aspects of life and not just our personal spiritual experiences. It is about demonstrating the Kingdom of God in all we do—how we conduct business, interact in our communities, and engage in relationships.

Sent like Jesus means we are dispatched into the world with a purpose and power similar to Christ. Our commission is not based on personal ambition but on divine sending. This distinction ensures that we operate not in our own strength but under the empowerment of the Holy Spirit, who guides and directs our actions to align with God's will.

It is crucial to remember that **the Holy Spirit guides us to our divine assignments**. We are not led by fleeting desires or the pursuit of personal gain but by a deep, continuous listening to the Holy Spirit's directions. This guidance ensures that our efforts are not only effective but also aligned with the eternal purposes of God.

Recognizing and responding to the Holy Spirit's communication is foundational in our walk as anointed believers. Our effectiveness in the Kingdom depends significantly on our sensitivity to His leadings. This dynamic interaction with the Holy Spirit ensures that we are always within the bounds of God's timing and will.

Obeying the Holy Spirit's promptings allows us to walk in God's power and authority. Each act of obedience is a step towards greater manifestations of the Holy Spirit's work in and through us, enabling us to tackle greater challenges and influence more lives for the Kingdom.

The manifestations of the anointing are as diverse as the needs we encounter. From preaching the gospel to setting the captives free, the Holy Spirit equips us uniquely for each task, ensuring that we carry out our heavenly mandates with divine efficacy.

Lastly, to **live out our identity as salt and light** effectively, we must continually immerse ourselves in the presence of God, allowing His Word and Spirit to fill us anew. This continual filling is what sustains us and enables us to be effective witnesses of His grace and power.

REFLECTIVE QUESTIONS

1. How do you actively live out your role as salt and light in your community?
2. In what ways have you experienced the Holy Spirit guiding you in your daily decisions?
3. How can you better respond to the Holy Spirit's promptings to ensure you are always walking in God's will?
4. What are some challenges you face in manifesting the anointing in your everyday life?
5. How can your understanding of being sent like Jesus influence your approach to ministry and daily living?

ACTIONABLE STEPS

- **Cultivate** an ongoing relationship with the Holy Spirit through daily prayer and meditation on God's Word to enhance your sensitivity to His guidance.
- **Equip** yourself with a deep knowledge of Scripture and a robust prayer life to ensure that you are always ready to respond to God's call with wisdom and authority.
- **Engage** in your community and spheres of influence with intentional actions that reflect God's love and righteousness, demonstrating the transformative power of the anointing in practical ways.

JOURNALING **Prompt**

Reflect on a recent experience where you felt you were being salt and light in your environment. How did you impact those around you, and what did you learn about living out your anointing more effectively?

$\sim$

CHAPTER 6

BAPTIZED IN FIRE

You are equipped with the Holy Spirit, not just for personal edification, but to empower you to act boldly in faith and witness. This is not a walk to take lightly; it is a charge to carry His fire wherever you go, transforming environments and setting hearts aflame with the love and truth of God. Luke 24:49 (NKJV)

"Behold, I send the Promise of My Father upon you; but tarry in the city of Jerusalem until you are endued with power from on high."

In **Chapter 6: Baptized in Fire**, I explore the profound and transformative experience of **Being Baptized in the Holy Spirit and Fire**. This baptism is not just a symbolic act; it is an all-encompassing immersion into the divine presence of God, affecting every aspect of our being. As we are drenched and engulfed in the Spirit, no part of us remains untouched by His power. This baptism signifies a life fully dedicated to God's purposes, showcasing a complete saturation of His presence.

Trust between the **baptizee and the baptizer** is essential, as it symbolizes our complete reliance on Jesus to not only immerse us in His Spirit but to also bring us safely through the process. This act of trust marks a pivotal point in our spiritual journey, confirming our faith in Jesus's role as our baptizer, who envelops us in the Holy Spirit and fire. It's an intimate act of surrender, acknowledging His authority and our dependence on His divine power.

Jesus's directives to His disciples to wait in Jerusalem until they were **endued with power from on high** underscores the importance of preparation and divine timing in our spiritual assignments. This waiting was crucial for the disciples, as it is for us; it ensures that we do not embark on our spiritual missions in our own strength but are equipped with the Holy Spirit's power, which is essential for effective ministry and witness.

The concept of baptism is multi-faceted, and **Understanding Different Baptisms** is crucial for our spiritual development. This understanding helps clarify our experiences and expectations of spiritual milestones. Whether it is being submerged in water or the Holy Spirit, each form of baptism has significant implications for our spiritual identity and mission.

The **Role of Fire in Baptism** goes beyond mere symbolism. It signifies the purification and empowerment necessary for our calling as Christians. Fire refines and energizes, representing the Holy Spirit's cleansing and empowering presence in our lives, preparing us to carry out God's will with boldness and purity.

On the day of Pentecost, the disciples experienced the **Immediate Evidence of Speaking in Tongues**, marking their baptism in the Holy Spirit. This sign was not only a fulfillment of prophecy but also a practical demonstration of the Spirit's power in their lives. Speaking in tongues empowered the disciples to break linguistic barriers and communicate the gospel across diverse cultures, exemplifying the Spirit's unifying power.

A true baptism results in a **Need for Complete Immersion** in the Spirit, where partial commitment gives way to a full surrender to God's call. This total immersion is transformative, marking us visibly and spiritually for God's service. It's about letting go of our reservations and diving deep into the depths of spiritual life that God calls us to explore.

In our mission as Christians, we are **Sent Like Jesus**, sent to serve and not to be served, equipped with the same Spirit that empowered Jesus. This divine commissioning carries with it the weight of responsibility and the honor of participating in God's redemptive work on earth, under the guidance and power of the Holy Spirit.

The **Connection Between Anointing and Fire** in our lives as believers is intended to be dynamic and visible. Our anointing should be characterized by passion, power, and the purposeful pursuit of God's kingdom on earth, reflecting His transformative power through our actions and interactions.

Lastly, the **Practical Outcomes of Spirit Baptism** demonstrate that this spiritual encounter is meant to transcend personal spiritual enrichment and extend to community and societal transformation. It equips us to perform 'good works' which are visible and beneficial, not just to the church but to society at large, showcasing the practical implications of our faith in real-world contexts.

In this chapter, as we delve into these themes, my hope is that you, as readers, will find clarity and encouragement to seek this profound experience of being baptized in the Holy Spirit and fire. This baptism is not an end in itself but a beginning of a life lived in full surrender and service to God, marked by His power and presence.

REFLECTIVE QUESTIONS

1. How does understanding the role of fire in spiritual baptism change your view of personal transformation?
2. What fears or hesitations might you have about being 'completely submerged' in the Holy Spirit, and how can you address them?
3. How can the trust relationship between you and Jesus as your baptizer deepen your faith?
4. In what ways can you practically prepare yourself to receive the baptism in the Holy Spirit as the disciples did?
5. What steps can you take to start witnessing with the power and anointing you receive from the Holy Spirit?

ACTIONABLE STEPS

- **Cultivate** an atmosphere of readiness and openness to the Holy Spirit's work in your life by daily prayer and surrender.
- **Equip** yourself with knowledge about the different aspects of spiritual baptism by studying scriptural examples and teachings.
- **Engage** in community and church activities where the baptism of the Holy Spirit is discussed and practiced, to gain firsthand experience and fellowship.

JOURNALING **Prompt**

Reflect on a moment in your life where you felt a powerful touch from God. How did it change you, and how can you seek a deeper immersion in His Spirit?

∾

RELEASING THE ANOINTING OFFICIAL WORKBOOK

CHAPTER 7

OUR PROGRESSION IN THE ANOINTING

Trust in the Lord with all your heart, and lean not on your own understanding; in all your ways acknowledge Him, and He shall direct your paths. (Proverbs 3:5-6)

As we journey through this chapter together, let us delve into the **divine order in anointing** that God has established for His people. Picture the oil, rich and flowing, starting from the head and cascading down Aaron's beard to the edges of his garments, as described in Psalms 133. This is not just a description of unity among brethren, but it signifies the meticulous nature of God's spiritual provisions, which begin at the highest leadership levels and flow down to touch every part of the Body of Christ. This pattern ensures that no part is neglected and each is sanctified and empowered to function in divine harmony.

Understanding the **progressive movement of the Spirit** can be likened to the growth of Jesus in wisdom and stature, as well documented in the scriptures. He did not receive His full capabilities at once; rather, He grew into them, as should we. This principle assures us that as we grow in our faith and understanding, the Spirit reveals more, allows us deeper insights, and equips us more fully. This progression is crucial as it prepares us to handle greater divine responsibilities and challenges, just as Jesus did from turning water into wine to raising Lazarus from the dead.

Reflect on the **miraculous progression** observed in Jesus' ministry, which teaches us about the readiness and timing in the spiritual realm. His first miracle, turning water into wine, was significant yet not life-threatening. It set a foundation. From there, His miracles grew in intensity and necessity, leading to the healing of the nobleman's son and eventually to the raising of the dead. Each step was a build-up, preparing Him and His disciples for the ultimate challenges of ministry. We too, are called to start where we are, use what we have, and expect to grow in miraculous works as our faith and spiritual understanding deepen.

Consider the **signs following believers** as a direct encouragement from Christ that our obedience and faith are not in vain. These signs—casting out demons, speaking in new tongues, and healing the sick—are not just proof of divine backing but are tools given to us to advance the Kingdom. They are designed to establish God's plan on earth and should be actively sought and practiced as part of our Christian walk.

The **nine manifestations of the Spirit**, which range from words of wisdom and knowledge to faith and healing, are not merely gifts but are essential tools for ministry. Each one serves a specific purpose in God's Kingdom to edify, to warn, to encourage, and to demonstrate God's power among His people. As you engage more deeply with these gifts, you're engaging with the very means by which God intends to spread His message and manifest His presence in the world.

In the **knitting of the Body of Christ**, we find our unique roles and functions. This isn't a random placement but a strategic positioning by the Holy Spirit. Just as every joint supports the body, every believer is positioned to support the growth and effectiveness of the Church. Your role, whether upfront or behind the scenes, is critical to the cohesive function and growth of the entire body.

When we speak of **growing in anointing**, it's akin to nurturing a plant from seed to full bloom. Our initial experiences with the Holy Spirit are seeds planted within us that need care, commitment, and nurturing. Regular engagement with God's Word, prayer, and fellowship are the water and sunlight needed. As you grow in your faith and understanding, so will your anointing. This growth allows you to carry more of God's power and presence, enabling you to do greater works.

Intimacy with God is the bedrock of effective ministry. Just like Mary, who treasured the words of the angel in her heart, our deepest revelations and instructions from God often come in quiet moments of profound connection with Him. Cherish these moments and guard the revelations given, for they are the blueprints of your ministry and calling.

The prophetic, kingly, and priestly anointing bestowed upon us is not for titles or show but for function. These anointings empower us to declare God's truth, to rule in the midst of our enemies, and to carry His presence wherever we go. Embrace these roles, for through them, you are called to impact lives and circumstances in the spiritual and physical realms.

Lastly, the **seed principle of growth** is a reminder that everything in the Kingdom starts small—from a word, a gesture, a prayer—and grows into something significant. Do not despise the days of small beginnings but see them as the starting point of a journey that leads to a rich harvest.

Through these reflections, I encourage you to deepen your engagement with the truths we've explored. Let each day be an opportunity to expand your understanding and experience of

God's anointing. As you grow, remember that every step forward is a step into greater realms of His power and love.

Reflective Questions

1. How does the concept of divine order in anointing influence your understanding of spiritual authority and responsibility?
2. In what ways can you actively engage with the progressive movement of the Spirit to ensure continuous spiritual growth?
3. How can the miraculous progression in Jesus' ministry inspire you to trust in the gradual development of your spiritual gifts?
4. Which of the nine manifestations of the Spirit do you feel most drawn to, and how can you cultivate a deeper relationship with that aspect of the Spirit's work?
5. What specific role do you believe God has for you within the Body of Christ, and how can you begin to function more effectively in that calling?

Actionable Steps

- **Cultivate an environment of growth** by setting aside regular times for prayer and meditation on the Word. This will water the seeds of the Spirit within you.
- **Equip yourself with knowledge** by studying the

lives of biblical figures who exemplified growth in their walk with God, such as Daniel or Paul.

- **Engage with the community of believers** in a way that uses your spiritual gifts. Whether through teaching, prophecy, healing, or service, find ways to actively participate in the life of your church or fellowship group.

JOURNALING **Prompt**

Reflect on a recent moment when you felt the Holy Spirit guiding or speaking to you. What was the context and how did you respond? Write about how this experience has impacted your faith and your willingness to follow the Spirit's lead in the future.

∼

_____
_____
_____
_____
_____
_____
_____
_____
_____
_____
_____
_____
_____
_____
_____
_____
_____
_____
_____
_____
_____
_____
_____
_____
_____
_____
_____
_____

OUR PROGRESSION IN THE ANOINTING

_____
_____
_____
_____
_____
_____
_____
_____
_____
_____
_____
_____
_____
_____
_____
_____
_____
_____
_____
_____
_____
_____
_____
_____
_____
_____

CHAPTER 8

REVERENCE AND OBEDIENCE: KEYS TO THE TANGIBLE ANOINTING

Keep your heart with all diligence, for out of it spring the issues of life. (Proverbs 4:23)

I n exploring **Reverence and Obedience**, we delve into the profound relationship between our spiritual maturity and the **tangible manifestation of the anointing**. Just as solid food is for the mature, who through constant use have trained their senses to discern both good and evil, so too is the deeper experience of God's anointing reserved for those who have cultivated a disciplined spiritual life. This chapter aims to unfold the critical roles of reverence and obedience in not only attracting but also sustaining the anointing in our lives.

Training our senses is not merely an intellectual exercise but a spiritual discipline. It requires us to actively engage with the Holy Spirit to refine our ability to discern God's voice from the noise of the world. This training enhances our spiritual perceptions, allowing us to discern the nuances of right and wrong according to God's standards. This is essential for anyone who desires to walk in a greater measure of the anointing.

The **tangible aspect of the anointing** serves as a bridge between the spiritual and the physical realms. It underscores the fact that spiritual truths have practical applications and manifestations. The anointing, while originating in the spiritual, is meant to have visible and tangible effects in the physical world —effects that advance God's kingdom and confirm His word.

Understanding the **maturity required to handle the anointing** is crucial. It is not a sudden acquisition but a progressive cultivation. We grow into it as we grow in our walk with God, much like Jesus grew in wisdom and stature. This maturity is marked by our capacity to handle spiritual responsibilities and challenges with discernment and integrity.

The power of the simple words **"yes" and "no"** in shaping our spiritual journey cannot be overstated. These words reflect our decisions to either align with God's will or reject the paths that lead away from it. They are the everyday expressions of our deeper choices about whom we serve and how we live out our faith.

Elisha's example in the **use of the anointing** during a crisis teaches us about the importance of spiritual preparation and the right conditions for the anointing to flow. His insistence on the right spiritual atmosphere, through the introduction of music, before he would prophesy, emphasizes that our environments and attitudes significantly impact the flow of the anointing.

The concept of **reverence** is foundational in our approach to God's presence. It is the deep respect and awe for God that should characterize our every action and decision. Reverence is what compels us to obedience and is what underpins a life that consistently reflects God's will and purpose.

The chapter also emphasizes that **obedience is the response required when the anointing is present**. Obedience activates the anointing and opens the door for God to work mightily through us. It is the practical outworking of our faith and reverence towards God.

Discerning the flow of the anointing, whether in times of quiet or in moments of overt spiritual activity, is key to moving in sync with the Holy Spirit. This discernment helps us to know when to act and when to be still, ensuring that our actions are always under the guidance of the Spirit.

Finally, the **importance of a correct response to the anointing**—whether in action or in reverence when the anointing is not manifest—is crucial for maintaining its flow in our lives. This correct response protects us from missteps that can quench the Spirit and hinder His work through us.

As you reflect on these insights, I encourage you to deepen your commitment to living a life of reverence and obedience. These are not merely virtues to be admired but practical keys that unlock deeper dimensions of God's power in your life.

REFLECTIVE QUESTIONS

1. How can training your senses help you in your spiritual walk?
2. In what ways can you cultivate a life that attracts and sustains the tangible anointing?
3. What does it mean to you to live a life of reverence towards God?
4. How does obedience influence the flow of the anointing in your life?
5. What steps can you take to ensure your environment is conducive to the flow of the anointing?

ACTIONABLE STEPS

- **Cultivate a disciplined prayer life** to enhance your spiritual sensitivity and discernment.
- **Equip yourself with scriptural knowledge** that reinforces the principles of obedience and reverence.
- **Engage in regular self-examination** to ensure your life aligns with the values of the kingdom, fostering an environment where the anointing can thrive.

JOURNALING **Prompt**

Reflect on a recent situation where you felt the need to exercise either reverence or obedience in response to the Holy Spirit's prompting. Write about the outcome of that situation and what you learned about the relationship between your actions and the flow of the anointing.

$\sim$

CHAPTER 9

JESUS BUILDS HIS CHURCH

"Be diligent to present yourself approved to God, a worker who does not need to be ashamed, rightly dividing the word of truth." (2 Timothy 2:15)

I n exploring how **Jesus continues His ministry through the Church**, we delve into the dynamic relationship between the anointing and the Church's role in the world. The Holy Spirit's outpouring on Pentecost was not only a pivotal moment in church history but also marked the beginning of an ongoing manifestation of Christ's work through His followers. This chapter aims to unfold the crucial roles of anointing in empowering believers for this divine mission.

The anointing's operation in our lives serves a dual purpose: it propels us into our divine destiny while ensuring we continue to grow spiritually. This dual function underscores that our effectiveness in the kingdom is not static but grows as we do. Each step we take in obedience and growth enables us to carry out our commission more effectively.

Understanding the **systematic function of the anointing**

helps us appreciate that spiritual growth and missional engagement are not random but part of a divine strategy. This system ensures that as we grow, we are equipped to undertake greater challenges and responsibilities in our Christian walk and ministry.

The concept of **revelation through communicative revelation** highlights that God designed humans to be conduits of His truth. The process of speaking and acting under the Holy Spirit's inspiration is the vehicle through which God's wisdom and nature are revealed on Earth, thereby countering the darkness with His light.

The anointing establishes righteousness and God's rule, reflecting a kingdom that not only displaces darkness but also actively establishes divine order. This transformative aspect of the anointing emphasizes that our battle is not only against spiritual darkness but also about positively shaping the spiritual landscape by establishing God's rule through righteousness.

The importance of **building up rather than merely tearing down** is critical in kingdom work. The same anointing that liberates from demonic oppression also empowers us to build robust spiritual lives. We must focus on nurturing and discipling those liberated to ensure lasting freedom and growth.

Jesus' role as the builder of the Church is foundational to understanding the Church's purpose and function. Through the revelation Peter received, which is that Jesus is the Messiah, the Son of the living God, we see that the Church is built on the revelation of Christ Himself—His identity, mission, and teachings.

This chapter also stresses that **the Church operates under a five-fold ministry** which mirrors the aspects of Christ's ministry: Apostle, Prophet, Evangelist, Pastor, and Teacher. These roles are not just titles but functional aspects of ministry that equip the saints, edify the body, and lead to maturity.

Spiritual maturity is required for handling divine assign-

ments effectively. Just as Jesus grew in wisdom and stature, believers are to grow into their spiritual roles, fully equipped and mature, able to handle the responsibilities and challenges of kingdom work.

Finally, the **church's mission extends beyond individual salvation to societal transformation.** As the Church embodies the fullness of Christ and operates under His governance, it influences and transforms communities and cultures, establishing God's kingdom on Earth as it is in Heaven.

REFLECTIVE QUESTIONS

1. How does understanding the systematic function of the anointing change your perspective on spiritual growth and ministry?
2. What role does communicative revelation play in your personal walk with God?
3. In what ways can you participate in both tearing down spiritual strongholds and building up the kingdom of God?
4. How can the five-fold ministry shape your understanding and involvement in the Church?
5. What steps can you take to grow into spiritual maturity to handle the responsibilities God has for you?

ACTIONABLE STEPS

- **Cultivate a deeper relationship with the Holy**

Spirit to understand and flow in the anointing more effectively.

- **Equip yourself with knowledge of God's Word** and how it applies to exercising kingdom authority.
- **Engage in building relationships within your church community** to foster mutual growth and support as you carry out your divine assignments.

JOURNALING **Prompt**

Reflect on the last time you experienced or observed the anointing in action within your church community. Write about this experience and how it impacted your understanding of the anointing's role in ministry and daily life.

∾

CHAPTER 10

ASSORTED ANOINTINGS ON ASSIGNMENT

Be steadfast in your faith and confident in the gifts God has placed within the Church. The diversity and functionality of these gifts ensure that the Body of Christ is fully equipped to fulfill its mission. Embrace the role you play in this divine orchestration, knowing that each part is crucial to the whole.

"For as we have many members in one body, but all the members do not have the same function, so we, being many, are one body in Christ, and individually members of one another." (Romans 12:4-5 NKJV)

In our journey as members of Christ's body, the Church, we are supported and guided by a divine structure known as the five-fold ministry. This framework is akin to **the hand of God**, where each finger represents a specific ministry—apostles, prophets, evangelists, pastors, and teachers. These roles are crucial, not just for the leadership but for the edification of the whole Church. Imagine trying to function without one of your fingers; similarly, the Body of Christ suffers if it lacks any one of these ministries. Their interconnected roles ensure a balance that is essential for the health and growth of the Church.

The anointing flows through believers as they operate in these roles, sourced from the Holy Spirit who equips each of us uniquely for our tasks. This spiritual empowerment is vital for the maturity and unity of the Church. It ensures that as we grow in our faith, we are also preparing to fulfill the great commission —going forth to make disciples of all nations.

However, it's important to recognize that **the balanced approach to ministry roles ensures no one is overburdened**. Not everyone is called to these ministry roles, but each believer can experience a touch of this anointing in their lives, contributing to the collective mission of the Church in various capacities. This balance helps prevent burnout and ensures that all members are functioning within their God-given capabilities.

Ephesians 4:13 highlights that these ministries are necessary until we all reach unity in faith and the fullness of Christ. This indicates that **the continuity of these ministries is necessary** for the Church to mature fully. Without the ongoing guidance and governance of these roles, the Church would struggle to achieve the stature of Christ as intended.

The cyclical relationship between growing, governing, and going forth in ministry underscores **the dynamic and interconnected nature of our callings**. Growth is not an isolated event but part of a continuum that feeds into and fuels further mission and governance. This dynamic ensures that as we mature spiritually, we are also increasingly effective in our witness and governance within the Church.

Within this system, each ministry has a unique function that contributes significantly to the overall effectiveness of the Church. For example, **each ministry has a unique function** that helps the Church to operate efficiently and effectively, addressing different needs within the Church and community.

Moreover, **diversity within each ministry** allows for a broader impact, reaching different people in ways that resonate with them specifically. This diversity is not just between the different types of ministries but also within each type. For instance, not all pastors will lead in the same way, and this variability allows them to connect with different segments of the congregation more effectively.

Understanding and respecting **the unique flow and emphasis of each minister** enhances how we receive from them. Knowing a pastor's or teacher's particular strength can help us better engage with their ministry, setting our expectations appropriately and enhancing our spiritual growth.

The collaborative approach is vital for leadership within the Church. **Interdependence among the ministries** shows that no single ministry can cater to all the needs of the Church. Rather, they must work in concert to effectively lead, nurture, and expand the Church's mission.

Ultimately, the goal of all these ministries is to **advance the Kingdom of God** by equipping believers and expanding the reach of the Church. This collective effort ensures the Church does not merely grow in number but deepens in faith, understanding, and commitment to Christ's mission on earth.

These ten key points encapsulate the profound and essential roles that the five-fold ministry plays in our lives as believers and members of the global Church. Each role, while distinct, is interconnected with the others, creating a robust system through which God governs, nurtures, and expands His Church. Through this divine setup, we are equipped not only to grow in personal faith but also to impact the world around us profoundly and enduringly.

REFLECTIVE QUESTIONS

1. How can you identify and engage with the different ministry gifts within your local church?
2. In what ways can you contribute to the balance and function of the Body of Christ, even if you are not called to a five-fold ministry role?
3. How does understanding the specific functions of each ministry role change your perspective on church leadership and involvement?
4. What steps can you take to foster a deeper appreciation and cooperation with the diverse ministries within your community?
5. How can the recognition of each ministry's unique role enhance your personal spiritual growth and the overall health of your church?

ACTIONABLE STEPS

- **Cultivate** a deeper relationship with members of your church who are in different ministry roles to understand their challenges and insights.
- **Equip** yourself with knowledge about the biblical foundation and practical implications of each of the five-fold ministries.
- **Engage** in church activities that support and enhance the functioning of these ministries, whether through volunteering, prayer, or active participation in their programs.

JOURNALING **Prompt**

Reflect on the interactions you've had with various ministry leaders. Consider how these interactions have shaped your understanding of church dynamics and your own spiritual growth. What can you do to be more supportive or engaged with these ministries?

~

CHAPTER II

THE FOUNDATION OF THE APOSTLES AND PROPHETS

Let us embrace the guidance of the apostles and prophets, recognizing that Jesus Christ is our chief cornerstone. This foundation is not just historical; it actively shapes our spiritual journey and collective growth. Embrace this truth, and let it inspire you to deeper faith and greater unity within your community.

Ephesians 2:20 (NKJV): "Having been built on the foundation of the apostles and prophets, Jesus Christ Himself being the chief cornerstone."

As we delve into the importance of the apostolic and prophetic foundations of the Church, it becomes clear that **the foundational role of apostles and prophets is rooted in the Scriptures**. This grounding is not merely historical but continues to influence us, providing stability and continuity within our faith community. Understanding this dual foundation helps us appreciate how the Word of God is both ancient and alive, directly influencing our daily spiritual lives and our collective church dynamics.

In examining this foundation, we see that **modern-day apostles and prophets bring stability and nourishment to the Church**. They serve as conduits of fresh insight into God's Word, ensuring that it remains relevant and fully applied to the challenges and changes we face today. This ongoing revelation does not add to the Scripture but helps us to apply its timeless truths more effectively in our modern context.

The operation of these gifts underlines that **apostolic and prophetic ministries are characterized by a submission to God's authority**. This submission is crucial because it aligns these ministries under Christ's lordship, ensuring that their authority and guidance are divine rather than self-generated. Through their leadership, structured in humility and reverence to God, the Church is shepherded towards unity and maturity.

The day-to-day impact of these ministries in our churches teaches us that **the anointing flows in fullness through divine order**. The structured flow of spiritual authority, from apostles and prophets through to pastors and teachers, ensures that the Church operates in harmony and effectiveness, guided by the Holy Spirit in a manner that is orderly and powerful.

This leadership is not about authoritarian control but about nurturing and guidance, where **the apostolic and prophetic offices require a relational rather than hierarchical approach to leadership**. This approach fosters a deeper, familial bond within the church community, where spiritual growth is supported through relationships built on mutual respect and love.

We also learn that **there is an interdependence of these ministries**, emphasizing the need for a cooperative approach to church leadership. This interconnectedness ensures that no single ministry dominates but rather that all work together to support and edify the church body in a balanced and holistic manner.

This balanced approach is essential because it enables the Church to **equip itself to navigate the challenges of modern ministry** effectively. By understanding and integrating the distinct roles and functions of each ministry, the Church can address a broader range of spiritual needs and community concerns with agility and depth.

Recognizing and respecting the roles of apostles and prophets within our community allow us to **engage with and benefit from the diverse ways God moves within His Church**. This engagement is crucial for personal growth and for the vitality of the church as a whole, ensuring that we are all nourished by the rich diversity of gifts that God bestows on His people.

These insights help underscore the importance of building our faith and our church life upon a foundation that is both robust and responsive—**a foundation that is ancient yet continually renewing**. As we align ourselves with this foundation, we are better equipped to face the future, secure in the knowledge that our faith rests on the solid bedrock of apostolic and prophetic truth, with Jesus Christ as the chief cornerstone.

Through this chapter, my hope is that you, the reader, will find a renewed appreciation for the apostolic and prophetic ministries within your own church setting. Understanding their biblical foundation and their current application will deepen your engagement with the Church and enhance your personal spiritual journey.

REFLECTIVE QUESTIONS

1. How do the apostolic and prophetic ministries in your church influence your spiritual growth?
2. In what ways does the teaching about the foundation of apostles and prophets challenge your current understanding of church leadership?
3. How can a better understanding of these ministries enhance your personal spiritual journey?
4. What steps can you take to engage more actively with the apostolic and prophetic voices in your community?
5. How does recognizing Jesus as the chief cornerstone affect your view of church unity and personal faith?

ACTIONABLE STEPS

- **Cultivate**: Begin a study group focused on the roles of apostles and prophets in the New Testament to deepen your understanding and appreciation of these foundational ministries.
- **Equip**: Attend workshops or seminars that focus on apostolic and prophetic teachings to enhance your capability to engage with and apply these insights in your local church setting.
- **Engage**: Actively participate in church activities that are led by apostolic and prophetic leaders to experience firsthand the richness and depth these ministries bring to the community.

JOURNALING **Prompt**

Reflect on your personal experiences with apostolic or prophetic ministries. How have these interactions shaped your understanding of God's plans for His Church and for your life? Write about how these revelations have changed or affirmed your spiritual path.

~

CHAPTER 12

THE GREATER ANOINTING

Stay committed to unity and purpose, as these are the
wellsprings of spiritual strength and corporate anointing.
Remember, the unity of the Church in spirit and truth is not
merely an ideal; it is a powerful reality that can significantly shift
the spiritual atmosphere.

**"Endeavoring to keep the unity of the Spirit in the bond of
peace." Ephesians 4:3**

I n my exploration of spiritual growth and unity, I've come
to realize that the **Corporate Anointing Power** is
profoundly impactful. Imagine the potential if we, the
Body of Christ, united as one. The glory that filled the Temple in
2 Chronicles 5 was not just a historical marvel; it stands as a
testament to what we can achieve together. This unity is what
the enemy seeks to disrupt because a united church is a powerful
bearer of God's glory.

Worship is a fundamental expression of our love and reverence for God. It isn't merely a song or a routine but a **Gateway to**

God's Presence. True worship elevates God, honoring His omnipotence and the completeness of Jesus' work on the cross. It isn't about catchy beats or lyrical prowess that stir the emotions but fail to stir the soul. True worship pulls us into a deeper communion with God, where we honor Him above all else.

In many of our gatherings, the role of the worship leader is pivotal. These leaders should have more than musical talent; they should possess a heart for leading us into God's presence. The goal is not to entertain but to facilitate a divine encounter. This **Role of Worship Leaders** is crucial; they must lead with a focus on God's presence, ensuring our worship time is not just another performance but a time of genuine spiritual engagement.

The Importance of Corporate Prayer is another area that deeply affects the spiritual atmosphere of our community. When we gather to pray, it's not to present a list of demands to God but to seek His voice and align our hearts with His divine will. In these moments, we're not just asking; we're listening, which transforms our gatherings into powerful sessions of divine strategy and alignment.

As I reflect on the practices of the early church, particularly their dedication to **Ministering to the Lord**, I am reminded of the power in simply adoring God. Their example in Acts shows us that our gatherings should focus on magnifying God, which naturally invites His guidance and presence into our midst.

This unity in prayer and purpose is essential. When we pray together with a single focus, as the early believers did, we create a powerful **Unity in Prayer** that can have a profound impact on our community and beyond. It's not about loudness or multitude but about the unity of hearts and minds in seeking God's will.

Through these practices, we exercise our **Spiritual Authority Through Worship and Prayer**. Worship becomes more than a song; it becomes a declaration of God's sovereignty and goodness. And as we engage in unified, Spirit-led prayer, we extend God's governance in the earthly realm, enacting His will through our collective voices.

One cannot overlook the **Anointing for Regional Impact**. Just as the apostles were empowered to reach diverse groups, we are called to impact our communities and beyond. This anointing doesn't just rest on the shoulders of the few; it's a collective mantle that we carry together as the Body of Christ.

The process of gathering in His name and under His anointing leads us to **Discipleship Through Corporate Engagement**. It is here, in the unity of worship and prayer, that we move from being mere followers to becoming disciples, embodying the teachings and character of Christ.

Lastly, the sustainability of this anointing is crucial. **Sustaining the Anointing Through Continuous Worship and Prayer** ensures that we remain in the flow of God's spirit. It's not a one-time event but a continual posture of worship and prayer that keeps us connected to the divine source.

Through these reflections and teachings, my hope is that you understand not only the significance of each aspect but also feel empowered to engage more deeply in your spiritual journey, enhancing your participation in the corporate life of the church and its mission in the world.

REFLECTIVE QUESTIONS

1. How can we more effectively foster unity within our church community to enhance the corporate anointing?

2. In what ways can worship leaders more deeply lead congregations into the presence of God rather than performing for them?

3. What role does individual preparation play in enhancing the effectiveness of corporate prayer?
4. How can we better recognize and encourage the different types of spiritual gifts and anointings within our church community?
5. What practical steps can we take to ensure that our worship and prayer are truly Spirit-led?

Actionable Steps

- **Cultivate** a personal prayer routine that aligns with seeking God's presence, not just His hand.
- **Equip** yourself and others by learning and teaching about the dynamics of spiritual authority and corporate anointing.
- **Engage** in creating more opportunities for the church to gather for prayer and worship, emphasizing unity and the collective pursuit of God's presence.

Journaling Prompt

Reflect on a recent worship or prayer experience. How did you feel God's presence? What might you change in your personal spiritual practices to enhance your sensitivity to the Holy Spirit during corporate gatherings?

Harrison House is a Spirit-filled, Word of Faith Christian publisher dedicated to spreading the message of faith, hope, and love through our wide range of inspiring publications. Committed to the messages that highlight the power of the Word and Spirit, we provide books, devotionals, and study guides that empower believers to live victorious, faith-filled lives.

Our resources are designed to help readers grow spiritually, strengthen their faith, and experience the transformative power of God's Word. Harrison House is passionate about equipping Christians with the tools they need to fulfill their divine purpose and impact the world for Christ.

www.ingramcontent.com/pod-product-compliance
Lightning Source LLC
Chambersburg PA
CBHW060425090426
42734CB00011B/2453